Is It an Insect?

by Isabel Thomas

What Are Insects?

Insects are small animals.

There are many different insects. They all have the same body parts.

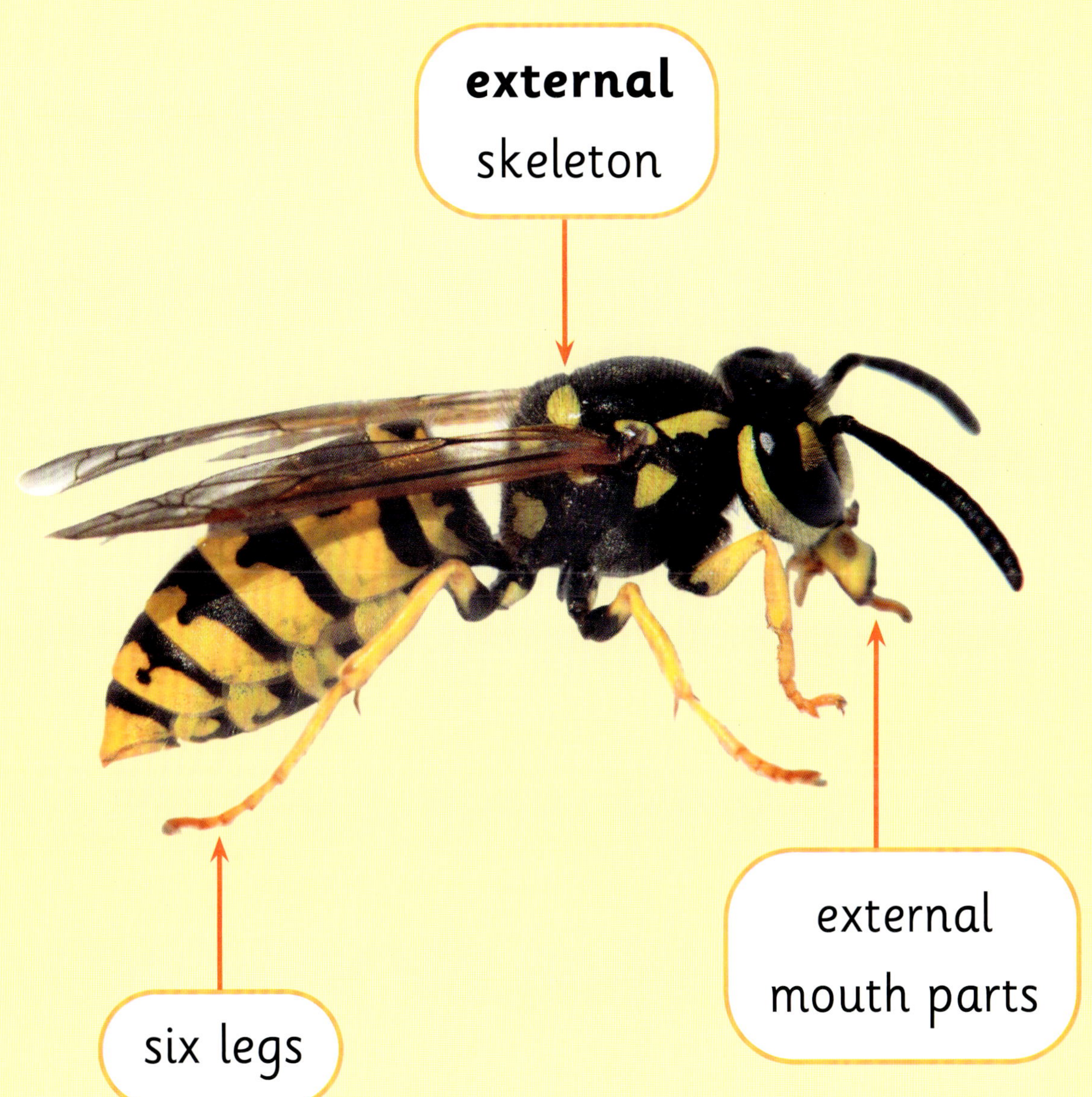

Spot the Insects!

Let's put your spotting skills to the test.

Is this an insect?

Yes! It's a beetle called a weevil. It walks on six legs. It has three body parts.

Sometimes it can be harder to tell. Is this an insect?

No! It's a springtail. It has six legs, but a soft body. It has **internal** mouth parts.

Nearly every insect has wings.

This animal has wings. Is it an insect?

Yes! It is a moth that looks like a hummingbird.

What do these insects **mimic**?

This critter has no wings! Is this an insect?

It is the **larva** of this spotty insect. It will grow wings once it is an adult.

Is this an insect?

Yes! It's an earwig. Its wings are under a hard case.

This creepy-crawly has an external skeleton. Could it be an insect with hidden wings?

No! It's a pill bug. It has 14 legs! It feeds on rotting wood.

A pill bug is not an insect. It is in the same family as prawns and lobsters!

Is this an insect?

It's a larva. A larva often looks completely different from the adult insect.

Is this an insect?

Yes! It's a water bug. Some adult insects hunt in water.

A water bug hunts fish and frogs to eat! They are a big meal.

Spotting Insects at Home

There are lots of insects to spot. You can help attract them to your garden.

Make a log pile.

Let weeds grow.

Dig a small pond.

Look It Up

external: on the outside

internal: on the inside

larva: insect that is not yet an adult

mimic: to copy or imitate

Index